Germany Coloring Book

FOR KIDS

inkHORSE Publishing

This Book belongs to:

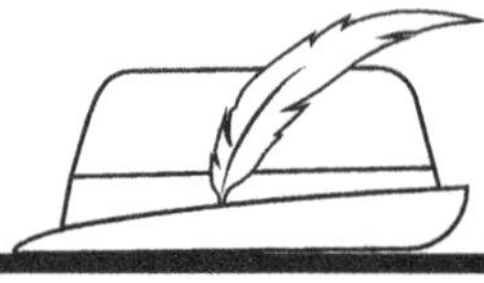

Munich

Best Festival
OKTOBERFEST

Nuremberg

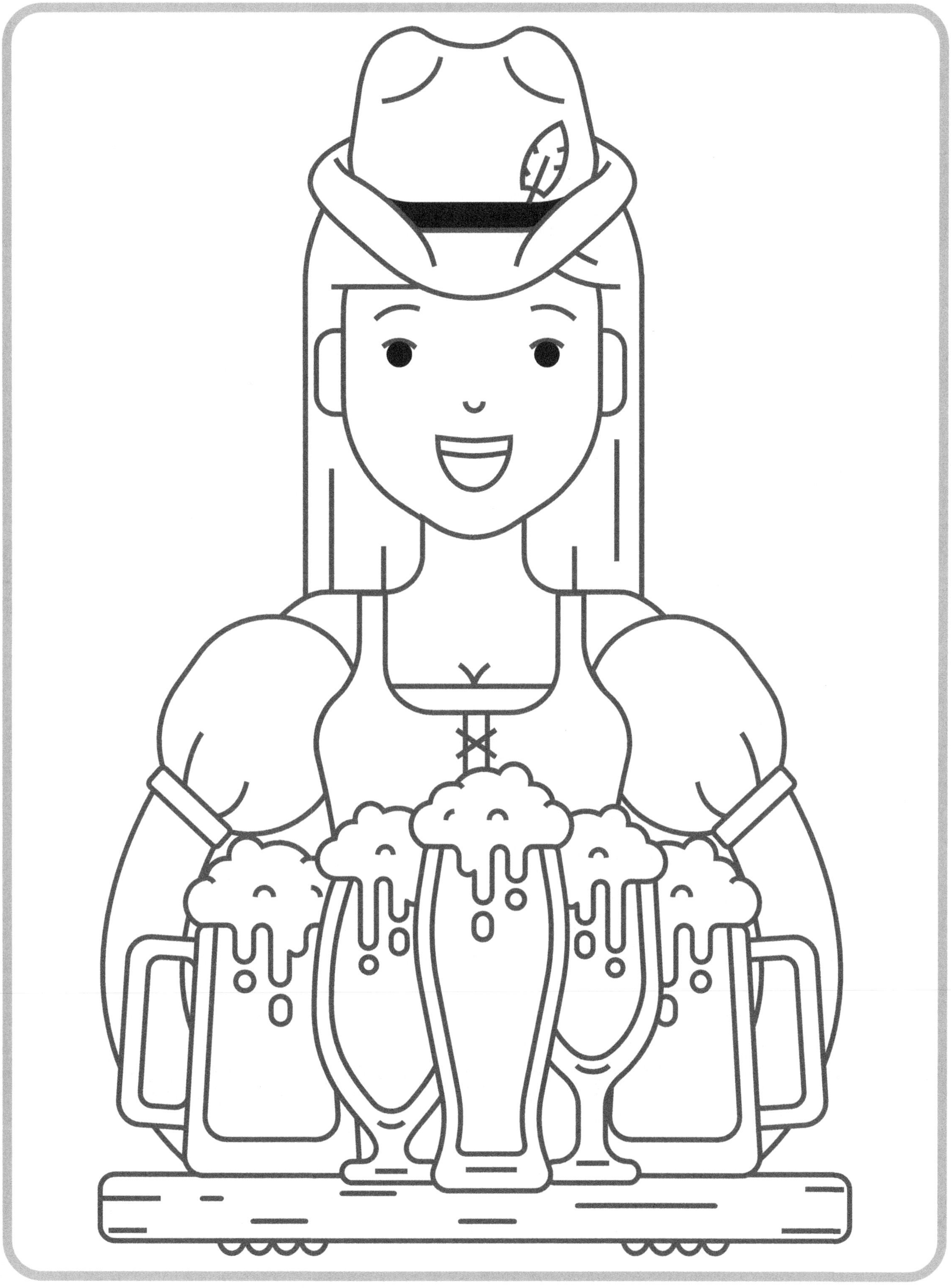

FOR MORE BOOKS SCAN THE QR CODE

Thank you!

inkHORSE Publishing

Made in the USA
Las Vegas, NV
23 November 2023

81373111R00037